The information in this book is purposes only. The Information is n(not constitute financial advice or any information is intended as inves   ui as a recommendation, endorsement, or sponsorship of any business, product or service. You are responsible for your own investment, purchase or other decisions.

With thanks to my wife Carla as my partner in crime and my friend Huyla Erdal for inspiring me to document my deeds.

chapter one

WHO'S THIS BOOK FOR?

Start small, but begin.
Anon

I have a confession to make: I murdered my mortgage. To make matters worse, I did it in a cold 7 years. In admitting my guilt to you I intend to inspire similar copycat crimes, hoping that you might commit the same deadly deed!

You'll be reading this book for a number of reasons I guess. You may be struggling with your mortgage, thinking 'I barely get by with my mortgage – how on earth did this guy pay it off in 7 years?' Or you might be someone looking to get on the housing ladder, seeing a mortgage as an insurmountable obstacle, but which a guy from Walthamstow (now a property hotspot) on a modest income has managed to wipe it out in a quarter of the time. You may be on the way to paying off your mortgage and want to learn from the lessons and pitfalls that I encountered on the way. Fact is, I didn't do everything right and I believe you can kill that mortgage even faster than me. This book will show you how I did it. In fact I want you to write me and tell me by how much you beat me!

I've always had a sense that paying off the mortgage as quickly as I could was something to strive for. Over the years I looked for various methods and went to a number of seminars to find out how, but always felt the schemes were too risky and I was suspicious of the motives of the organisation or person who devised the system. You're usually required to invest in this, pay to attend that and sell the other. Sorry, not for me. There are other approaches and I'm not saying they don't work, but here's mine: a straightforward common sense method without smoke, mirrors or risk. At the very least this book will show you that it can be done without trickery, if you didn't believe previous to reading this that it could be done. But it's more than that – it's more than the financials. It's also a mindset. A very deliberate mindset.

Before we get down to business, a quick word about who this book is NOT for. This book is not for anyone with serious financial and debt problems. I'd probably seek help from organisations like CAP (Christians Against Poverty) or the Citizens Advice Bureau for debt advice.

In researching books already out there on this subject, the most popular appears to be a book written to accompany a TV series. There are others that claim you can pay your mortgage off in 2 minutes. I like self-help books, but it seems to me that many of them are written by wealthy people. I'm not a rich guy or TV presenter. For someone like you starting out on this path, buying a typical flat or an average sized house, I'm not sure I could identify with the advice of millionaires - I am sure they buy their houses quite easily thank you very much! I'll show you my income, mortgage statements and other documents which I think you'll find interesting. I'll prove to you that I've actually done it*!*

My nephew Arran says he admires my ambition because I have a number of ideas that I generally follow through on (blush)! He suggests that this book has educative value for young teens, showing them a better way to think about money and achieve their goals. Alternatively it could be that you're reading this book because you can taste the freedom of that distant dream: a life without a mortgage. Or you may just be curious about my story.

So here goes...

chapter two

MY STORY

> *"Lock 'em arf!"*
>
> George Cornelius

I come from an ordinary working class background. I recall, in the days when passports contained a person's occupation, that my father's said 'Labourer' – he worked as an injection moulder in a toy factory named 'Britains'. My mother spent most of her working career as a cleaner. I'm the middle child of a larger than average five and so money was tight. It's no surprise that my father was always keen to save money. We would receive a fearful telling-off for leaving the lights, TV or gas flame heater on in empty rooms. "Lock 'em arf", he would snarl (Caribbean slang meaning 'turn it off'). My father would never pay anyone to do any work on the house – installing our own central heating or building a kitchen extension virtually by himself (I had to hold and fetch various things, often in the cold, which I hated). Does this explain why I have the same tendencies?

As a child I was a keen saver. My mum opened a TSB account with just £5 when I was maybe 5 years of age. There it stayed earning a few pennies in interest for years. In secondary school I added to it with money from my three paper rounds. Soon I had around £100 in the account. I was devastated, however, to see that it still earned only a few pence interest. I promptly closed the account and bought Lyle & Scott and Pringle golfing jumpers and light blue Farah trousers, such was the teenage fashion at the time!

Unlikely as it was for someone with my background, after a long-winded route I found my way to university to study Economics. Statistics was my worst subject and so I gave up, preferring to daydream in that final exam of a way to accumulate vast wealth in a short period of time, based on what I read in a sociology book some years earlier: interest on top of interest is the way the rich get richer. Thinking about the subject of this book, it's also one way the poor get poorer.

After university I worked for a small IT company earning around £18,000 a year. I had modest increases over the years as I changed jobs. One pattern I can see is that I continued my interest in saving. Thanks to this habit I gathered together a £23,000 deposit for our house.

I have a typical family: a wife and two kids. With each birth my wife made the decision to spend the first 2 years of their life dedicated to raising them. When she did work, it was mostly part-time and definitely below the national average wage. In all this I suppose I'm trying to say that I'm a pretty average Joe. So how did I pay off my mortgage in 7 years with no gimmickry or high risk shenanigans?

chapter three

MOTIVATION

"The statistics on sanity are that one out of every four people is suffering from a mental illness. Look at your 3 best friends. If they're ok, then it's you."

Rita Mae Brown

Before we get down into the detail, let's have a think about why you'd want to pay your mortgage off in a quarter of the time. If that seems a silly question, why is it that the majority of people don't? I have my reasons, but before I tell you mine, it might be useful to consider your motives. What are your reasons for wanting to kill your mortgage?

1. _____

2. _____

3. _____

For me there were a number of reasons, but I suppose the first of these is that I am not insane. Take a look at this:

5. Overall cost of this mortgage	
The overall cost takes into account the payments in Sections 6 and 8 below. With a repayment mortgage you gradually pay off the amount you have borrowed, as well as the interest, over the life of the mortgage.	
The total amount you must pay back, including the amount borrowed is:	£390,659.22
This means you pay back:	£1.86 for every £1 borrowed
The overall cost for comparison is:	5.7% APR

Do you understand what this means? It means that if I pay off my mortgage over the agreed full term of 25 years I will pay nearly £2 for every £1 borrowed. In 2006 I borrowed £210,000. If I take the full 25 years to pay the loan back making the agreed monthly minimum payment of £1311.72, all told with interest I would end up paying the bank back nearly £400,000. Carla astutely commented that this affects the actual profit you'll make if you sell the house. Don't curse the banks – hell they've got to make their money somehow! You don't have to be a genius, however, to see that to pay the bank back double what I borrowed is not a good deal for me and I'm not that insane.

I've always hated the idea paying back the loan company much more than I borrowed, with a passion. Look at this:

ARRRGHHH*!!!* Goods cost = £541.65; pay back £1076.40. A high interest rate was not the problem, of course, with my bank loan: it was just debt interest building up on debt interest over a number of years. In summary therefore, I did not want to pay the bank back double what they lent me, on principle.

The second reason I wanted to kill my mortgage as quickly as I could was security. I always sneered when people said: "I bought a house". This to me implies that like a pair of trainers you bought the house and you *own* it. You don't own your house - the bank do! You don't own that property until you've paid the bank all their money. If you can't pay them, it's theirs.

> **7. Are you comfortable with the risks?**
>
> **What if interest rates go up?**
> The monthly payments shown in this offer document could be considerably different if interest rates change. For example, for one percentage point increase in the HSBC variable rate, your monthly payments will increase by around £122.44.
>
> *Rates may increase by much more than this so make sure you can afford the monthly payment.*
>
> **What if your income goes down?**
> You will still have to pay your mortgage if you lose your job or if illness prevents you from working. Think about whether you could do this.
>
> *Make sure you can afford your mortgage if your income falls.*
>
> The FSA's information sheet 'You can afford your mortgage now, but what if... ?' will help you consider the risks. You can get a free copy from www.fsa.gov.uk/consumer or by calling 0845 456 1555.

Security is important. You have a mortgage. You lose your job, or your partner does or you lose your income in some other way. These things happen and they're not always predictable. What's pretty much the first thing you panic about? Is it your car, your lifestyle or the annual holiday abroad? Hell no, it's your mortgage! Interest rates are low in 2015 and presumably must rise at some point as the economy improves, making for higher repayments. I noticed, however, that people are in no real rush to pay off their mortgages, preferring to buy expensive cars, take foreign holidays and the like.

The Great Mortgage Mystery

I'll never be able to fathom this one. It's November 2008 and we're just starting into a recession. What's the thing most homeowners fear in a recession? Repossession. Anyone out there actually love getting out of bed to do the daily commute and endure 8 hours of slavery?

Thought not, but you do it for the mortgage. Well then why the hell don't you put everything you've got into paying off that mortgage and getting rid of that bitch ASAP? I just don't get it. One of the greatest threats, but they seem to want to prolong it.

And people seem to want to make it worse by buying the most expensive house they can cos they just have to live in that exclusive area with the best schools, as if it really matters that much. It would be great to live in Islington, but for me the cost in terms of wasting my life working for someone else is just too high.

We have a Skoda. I like our Skoda. Our Skoda is second-hand. Many people have BMWs and other nice cars. I would love an Audi or BMW. The people in BMWs might look at us in our Skoda and think, "Ha – could only afford a Skoda eh?" Not actually – we could afford a much better car and other frivolous things, but we're not stupid enough to add another 5+ years to our mortgage, paying the bank nearly £2 for every £1 borrowed. Let's say that in a different way: borrow £200,000 and pay the bank back £400,000. My advice: get a tracker with a low rate or anything that allows unlimited overpayments and get rid of that monster as soon as you can.

Imagine the freedom! Choose when you want to work. You could work half a day or work half the week or take 6 months off each year. Don't like your work anymore? Tell your company to go jump and look for something else…or don't look for something else! Watch films all day, work on that genius idea, spend more time with your kids, read your favourite books, visit the world.

Nope, you'd prefer to eat out, buy big cars and take expensive holidays. Enjoy your sweaty commute and sweat out the recession. I'll be on the beach.

Orall Cornelius 2008

Forgive me – I was younger, angrier and extremely opinionated back then (still am)*!* But that partly summarises the mindset outlined in this book. As I've indicated in that piece, the third reason you'd want to kill your mortgage quickly is freedom. When you're young you swallow the company spiel, are willing to travel anywhere and work all hours. As you get older, less so. You realise there's more to life. Don't think so? If you died tomorrow, ask yourself, would your company care? The painful truth is no. You'll be office gossip for a few days and some may attend your funeral, but you know their key concern would be getting someone to deal with your workload. Does killing yourself for the company look like sense having read that?

Point is that as you get older your priorities may well change. Mine have. I have lots of other things I want to pursue: writing, saxophone playing, rowing, film making. Working to pay the mortgage is not how I want to spend my time at this point in my life. My dad did it that way but I'm doing it different. Now that I'm feeling the impatience of the mid-life crisis there are lots of other things I want to achieve before my time's up. Time is short, so let's get to it!

chapter four

SETTING THE SCENE

Sometimes it is the people no one imagines anything ofthat do the things no one can imagine.

The Imitation Game

In the two years after I finished university in 1995 I worked for Manpower, the temping agency. As you can imagine, the hourly pay was nothing to speak of. I remember, though, that I still managed to put some money away in unit trusts (PEPs, not ISAs, were the tax saving scheme at the time), believing that it would be the path to riches. It wasn't, so don't worry, it was not really part of the path to paying off my mortgage quickly.

I had a break when a university friend of mine put his foot in the door for me at his IT company, remembering that I had a background in computing. This meant a salary of £18,000, which for me at the time was significant. It wasn't a vast sum, but my lifestyle changed. The job was in Aylesbury and so I moved from Walthamstow and started paying rent. I remember being very proud of my gold card and started flashing it around, especially to my girlfriend Carla (she remembers that too)!

As an aside, I remember that Carla and I got together at a time when I was moving forward in the world and sublimely happy being independent. I recall often going to the cinema on my own and thinking it was perfectly normal. It wasn't until years later that I realised it wasn't really the thing to do and that one must go to the cinema with friends! My learning from that was that a person is at their most attractive when they see excitement in life, can enjoy their own company and are moving forward.

I left that job when I realised that I was surrounded by IT contractors earning £40 per hour (over £70000 a year perhaps) who couldn't do the job half as well as me on £18,000. I shocked my company and others around me, when left to go contracting (wouldn't you leave?) It opened the floodgates and soon the other employees left also!

It was a short stint of only 6 months or so until I started work for Enron. Perhaps you remember the giant US energy company that exaggerated profits and concealed debts, finally going into bankruptcy? Here I was on around £55,000 a year (together with a £10,000 golden handshake). It was a great company to work for with fantastic benefits - like a candy store in terms of me getting anything I wanted. Maybe that was part of its downfall! Anyway I think I took on more than I could handle there and left after 9 months for something more on my level. I had to pay back some of that handshake in case you're wondering!

Working for Ogilvy Interactive, part of the advertising agency, was fun but chaotic. I was on £35,000 at that

Oxford Street digital agency, where I worked for a year until I got married to Carla in the year 2000. When we returned from our honeymoon I did a couple IT contracts, but on lower rates than before. I decided to take a year out in 2003 to work on an invention that I had wanted to bring to market for some time, named 'The Gentleman's Friend'. I challenge you to find out what it was: you'll be surprised! That also was a lot of fun but drained finances as I funded it myself with savings and still had to pay for rent and food etc. Carla was working for a Park Lane hotel on the switchboard and while she worked hard, she did not bring in a very significant amount of money, as you can imagine. She left to set up her own business making clothes for the residents of Walthamstow which brought in even less money and more sporadic.

In 2003 Carla was pregnant with our first child so I had to stop what was perhaps one of the most fulfilling ventures of my life to get a proper job. I had managed to design and bring to market the Gentleman's Friend Ltd products and services, but despite some sales it was losing money. So I started work for EDF Energy in the month before our daughter was born. The salary was £35,000.

In summary, while my income had some ups, it also had some downs and you can see that I started at EDF Energy on an income the same or lower than other positions I've had in the past. Why? I took that position for the security - I figured that people always need electricity. I recall rejecting the offer of IT jobs in the finance sector in favour of EDF Energy and looking at 2008 I was right. Didn't feel it at all. In fact 2008 presented opportunities, but more on that later.

The point of all this is that if you look at it, I didn't have an extraordinary income. In fact I reckon a person starting work at 21 moving from job to job and steadily increasing their income could probably have matched or even surpassed the total income generated by Carla and I in our patchy career history. If you're part of a couple I stand doubly by that sentiment! I was shocked by a couple on BBC Question Time, who were both accountants, who said they couldn't afford to buy a home. Lots of couples can do this and I plan to show you how.

I said earlier that my savings were not really part of the path to paying off our mortgage quickly and that's true. Savings were part of the path, however, to actually getting a mortgage and a property. Despite depleting savings with my year out, we still had around £25,000 left. The three bedroom house we bought in Walthamstow in 2006 cost £233,000 and I put down a deposit of £23,000. So I got a mortgage of £210,000. A lesson from that I suppose is that it's a good habit to put away money, even if you see no immediate need to do so. I'm in disbelief when I hear of couples on good money who say they can't get together a deposit for a house. I'll cover an approach for doing that later, including the only sure way I know to make money from the stock market.

The surveyor said the cost of the house was on the pricey side compared to the market in Walthamstow. A lesson there was that we underestimated our power as first time buyers. For people in a chain that I learned had fallen through a few times previously, a solid first time buyer with a good deposit can be a godsend. I look back and think I should've taken the risk of bargaining harder. This might depend on the market though. So buying cheap was not part of the path to paying off the mortgage quickly either.

Thinking back though, we had our second child on the way, Carla really wanted to get something and the sellers could sense it. Sometimes when you look back you think yourself an idiot for the choices and decisions you've made. It's important not to blame yourself: you did the best that you could given the situation, perceived pressures and your state of mind at that the time. Another life lesson. I rate my house as nearly the worst purchase of my life for that reason; but our first car bought soon after - a Fiat Punto bought privately for £2,000 when I knew nothing about cars - had to be my worst. It lasted 6 months. For the least hassle if you know nothing about cars, go to a reputable dealer. (I didn't even take it for a test drive!) Another life lesson.

So we've seen what wasn't part of the equation in murdering the mortgage – savings, investments and house prices. Let's take a look at what was.

chapter five

THE MORTGAGE

A newbie to the housing game, I can't really remember the basis on which I chose my mortgage. It was being offered by my bank of 10 years and they were generous in terms of the loan to value (the ratio of the value of the house vs how much I wanted to borrow) and my income at the time.

4. Description of this mortgage

We, HSBC Bank plc, are pleased to provide you with an offer document for an HSBC mortgage.

- You will be borrowing £210,000.00.
- The mortgage will be at a variable rate, currently 5.75%, with a discount of 1.26% for 2 years from the date the funds are drawn down, giving a current rate payable of 4.49%.
- HSBC's standard variable rate, currently 5.75% applies after this discount rate period ends for the remaining term of the mortgage. We call this the HSBC variable rate.
- This mortgage is available if you have graduated in the last five years.

Any changes to the rates will take effect immediately. We will give you notice of any change in your monthly payment.

As you can see it had a fairly good rate in comparison to what was around at the time, as it included a discount for 2 years. In exchange for this deal I had to pay a booking fee of £399 and a valuation fee of £195, which wasn't too bad in comparison to the rest of the market. Two key things to note about this mortgage was firstly that it was a variable rate mortgage, meaning that the rate could go up, normally with a change in the Bank of England base rate.

> **7. Are you comfortable with the risks?**
>
> **What if interest rates go up?**
> The monthly payments shown in this offer document could be considerably different if interest rates change. For example, for one percentage point increase in the HSBC variable rate, your monthly payments will increase by around £122.44.
>
> *Rates may increase by much more than this so make sure you can afford the monthly payment.*

That would mean a higher monthly payment and that was a risk, as you can see in my mortgage agreement document. The key drawback of this mortgage, however, was that during the first 2 years - the discounted rate period - there was a limit on the amount I could pay back above the agreed monthly repayment amount: in other words a limit on overpayments. The key to paying off your mortgage early is to put any spare cash you have into the mortgage to reduce the capital and total interest, but this mortgage imposed a limit on that. In fact it would penalise you if you tried.

10. What happens if you do not want this mortgage any more?

Early repayment charges

- You will be liable to pay us an early repayment charge when you repay the whole or any part of the mortgage, over and above your standard monthly payments, during the discount rate period.
- The charge is 1% of the amount repaid early for each remaining year of the discount rate period, reducing on a daily basis.

Date of repayment	Cash example
20 July 2006	£4,205.75
20 July 2007	£2,059.24
20 June 2008	£165.17

The maximum charge you could pay is £4,205.75.

You can understand this, because as I said earlier, on a deal like this the bank have to make their money somehow! What should you do with your income that can't be used to make overpayments? That depends on your circumstances. I'll cover the specifics later, but obviously if you can afford it you should invest or save it. With a new house, a child and a second on the way though, you can imagine that there were other expenses to take care of.

As I said, I was locked into this mortgage for 2 years with a penalty for attempted escape! During those two years, however, I was plotting my deadly attack on the mortgage. The day would come when I was free to roam and move my mortgage anywhere. I stalked the market for the best deals. A bit savvier now, I was looking for 2 key things:

1. The lowest interest rate

2. Ability to make unlimited overpayments

This meant that fixed rates were out of the window as, although they offered security, they restricted overpayments and their interest rates were higher than variable rate deals. In order to obtain the two criteria I mentioned I was willing to pay any booking fee, as I knew it would pay off in the long-term. I might add that I wanted a deal where I could escape without penalty if later on I found something better, but this was subordinate to the 2 points above. Offset mortgages (which allowed unlimited overpayments and counted savings as though they reduced the capital sum and therefore reducing total interest) were attractive but had higher rates and so were out for me.

The answer came in the form of a tracker mortgage. This tracked the Bank of England base rate, which at the time was 5.00, plus 0.79%. Again, there was a risk of a rate increase as before, but this time it was a direct link (whereas with variable rate mortgages there's usually a short pause before a change). I don't believe I had a view on the direction of interest rates, I just hoped they wouldn't go up too steeply too soon.

---

4. Description of this mortgage

We, HSBC Bank plc, are pleased to provide you with an offer document for an HSBC mortgage.

- You will be borrowing £196,969.63.

- The mortgage will be at a variable rate which is 0.79% above the Bank of England base rate, currently 5.00%, to give a current rate payable of 5.79%. Any changes to the rate as a result of a Bank of England base rate change will take effect the day after that change.

We will give you prior written notice of any consequential change in your monthly payment.

This is probably the greatest risk there is with my approach. From memory this probably wasn't the cheapest deal out there - HSBC and others were offering discount mortgages like the one I was on previously - but

I have discussed the disadvantages of those already. As a bonus there was no booking fee as I was a preferred customer and there was no valuation required as they did the valuation two years previously. You can also see that by this point with the previous deal I had paid off around £13,000 in 2 years. The annual statement below shows that this had started to have an impact on the amount of interest paid each month.

HSBC

3
Mr Cornelius
20 July 2008

Date	Payments Due	Payments Received	Payments and Interest Applied
21 December 2007	£1,301.98		
21 December 2007		£1,562.36	
21 December 2007			£952.10
21 January 2008	£1,265.43		
21 January 2008		£1,562.36	
21 January 2008			£942.28
21 February 2008	£1,263.56		
21 February 2008		£1,518.50	
21 February 2008			£935.25
21 March 2008	£1,263.56		
25 March 2008		£1,518.50	
25 March 2008			£853.19
26 March 2008			£1.21
21 April 2008	£1,231.08		
21 April 2008		£1,477.26	
21 April 2008			£887.49
21 May 2008	£1,231.08		
21 May 2008		£1,477.26	
21 May 2008			£839.62
21 June 2008	£1,199.37		
23 June 2008		£1,439.24	
23 June 2008			£839.59

Think of that though: if I paid in £1500, around £900 of that was gone in interest and so the capital sum was only reduced by £600. Who would want to sustain that situation? Even more motivation for reducing the capital. It was going to be a long haul, but the chipping away of the capital and subsequent reduction in interest gave me hope! I was making the maximum overpayment that I could without incurring penalty, paying around £250 more each month than I had to. I didn't always get it precisely right though.

Fees and Charges

The following fees and/or charges have been debited to your mortgage during the period of this statement.

Date	Description	Amount
26 March 2008	MTGE PAYMENT FEE	£1.21

OOPS!

A dramatic shock to the economy took place. The financial crisis caused panic and gave rise to the 'credit crunch'. Interestingly, given the subject of this book, it was caused by a rise in US interest rates, which caused already squeezed homeowners to default on their mortgages. Cutting the story short, a global slowdown in economic growth was predicted and central banks cut interest rates dramatically to stave off a slump into recession.

Bank of England Base Rate Changes

Thu, 10 Apr 2008, 5.0000
Wed, 08 Oct 2008, 4.5000
Thu, 06 Nov 2008, 3.0000
Thu, 04 Dec 2008, 2.0000
Thu, 08 Jan 2009, 1.5000
Thu, 05 Feb 2009, 1.0000
Thu, 05 Mar 2009, 0.5000

Source: Bank of England

What did this mean for me? You'll remember that I switched to a tracker mortgage that tracked the Bank of England base rate plus 0.79%. This means the interest rate on my mortgage went from 5.79% to 1.29% in less than a year. Let's look at the effect that had on my mortgage over that same period.

Date	Type	Description	Paid out	Paid in	Balance (£)	
23 Sep		Balance brought forward			194370.02	D
29 Sep	TFR	173877 17533018		650.00	193720.02	D
01 Oct	TFR	173877 17533018		730.02	192990.00	D
21 Oct	CR	MORTGAGE PAYMENT		1439.24		
21 Oct	DR	DEBIT INTEREST	888.77			
21 Oct	TFR	173877 17533018		874.53	191565.00	D
21 Nov	CR	MORTGAGE PAYMENT		1439.24		
21 Nov	DR	DEBIT INTEREST	750.46			
21 Nov	TFR	173877 17533018		176.22	190700.00	D
19 Dec	TFR	173877 17533018		675.00	190025.00	D
22 Dec	CR	MORTGAGE PAYMENT		1439.24		
22 Dec	DR	DEBIT INTEREST	510.35		189096.11	D
10 Jan	TFR	173877 17533018		74.00	189022.11	D
21 Jan	CR	MORTGAGE PAYMENT		1439.24		
21 Jan	DR	DEBIT INTEREST	417.02			
21 Jan	TFR	173877 17533018		139.89	187860.00	D
03 Feb	TFR	173877 17533018		215.00	187645.00	D
20 Feb	TFR	173877 17533018		320.00	187325.00	D
23 Feb	CR	MORTGAGE PAYMENT		1439.24		
23 Feb	DR	DEBIT INTEREST	326.56		186212.32	D
06 Mar	TFR	173877 17533018		88.32	186124.00	D
20 Mar	TFR	173877 17533018		2177.00	183947.00	D
23 Mar	CR	MORTGAGE PAYMENT		1439.24		
23 Mar	DR	DEBIT INTEREST	217.42		182725.18	D
21 Apr	CR	MORTGAGE PAYMENT		1439.24		
21 Apr	DR	DEBIT INTEREST	200.28			
21 Apr	TFR	173877 17533018		804.22	180682.00	D
02 May	TFR	173877 17533018		130.00	180552.00	D
21 May	CR	MORTGAGE PAYMENT		1439.24		
21 May	DR	DEBIT INTEREST	191.49			

You should be looking in the 'Paid Out' column. What a dramatic difference! The decision to take a tracker mortgage paid off. From paying nearly £900 in interest, after the rate cuts I was paying under £200 in interest. What's the significance? I was transferring roughly £2300 into the mortgage account each month (look for 'TFR' in the Type column) and only £200 was eaten up in interest. This means the capital amount was being reduced by a massive £2100 each month. After transferring the same amount previous to the rate falls the capital amount was only being reduced by £600, my hard earned being annihilated by interest. Over the 7 month period in the previous statement the mortgage was reduced by about £4300. The change in mortgage and interest rates meant that over a 7 month period in the second statement the mortgage fell by £13000.

Writing this section I asked myself if I was fortunate that I had this rate fall, meaning that what I've done could only be achieved in specific favourable circumstances. For two reasons: No. Firstly the principle of making maximum overpayments for a faster finish is straightforward and always works. Secondly we threw away money (by not budgeting for example) meaning that even if you faced a higher interest rate than me, better budgeting would mean that you could match or beat me. Moreover a quick look shows me that you have the same opportunity that we had in that mortgage rates are pretty low in 2015, particularly if you have a good deposit.

I said earlier in this section that my criteria for choosing my new mortgage was (a) the lowest interest rate and (b) the ability to make unlimited overpayments. Exception: if you can only find a little extra to make overpayments each month then go for the lowest rate. Doing a quick search, these are mortgages that start with an initial discount for 2 years and will probably allow some limited overpayments. Make sure you can get out of them when the special offer is over. But my big bone is that almost anyone can find extra cash for overpayments or money for a deposit. That's the other part of the equation and that's what the next section is all about.

chapter six

SAVING MONEY

A moment of pain is worth a lifetime of glory!

Pete Zamperini

I started with a large deposit and was able to transfer a sizeable amount of money each month (over £2000 and still more when Carla's career really started to fly) to the mortgage account because I kept a control of expenses.

As you saw from my piece 'The Great Mortgage Mystery' I believe that people spend money on things that they can't really afford to when they have a mortgage debt. You might say, "well I think it's necessary to have a top of the range £20,000+ car - it fits my lifestyle and you who are you to tell me it's not necessary? I can afford it so I'm a gonna buy it!" Yes you're right.

I studied Economics at university and I came across something called 'opportunity cost' in relation to the subject of scarcity. It's the basis of Economics. Scarcity means that we have to make choices. Opportunity cost means that if we make a certain choice we have to forego something else. If my salary for the month is £1 and I have a choice between a £1 pizza and £1 hamburger and

I choose pizza, I forego the hamburger. What does this mean in relation to your mortgage? If I buy a £20,000 car the opportunity cost is money towards your mortgage. Reducing the money towards your mortgage equates to an increased time to the end date. I think of it like this: each £1 taken away from the mortgage and spent elsewhere means an extra 1 day on your mortgage. I've still to work out the precise increase in days, but the principle is obviously true and that's how I think about it. The clock is ticking on your mortgage: more time means more interest which means more time. So if you're going to spend money on other things, make sure it's worth it.

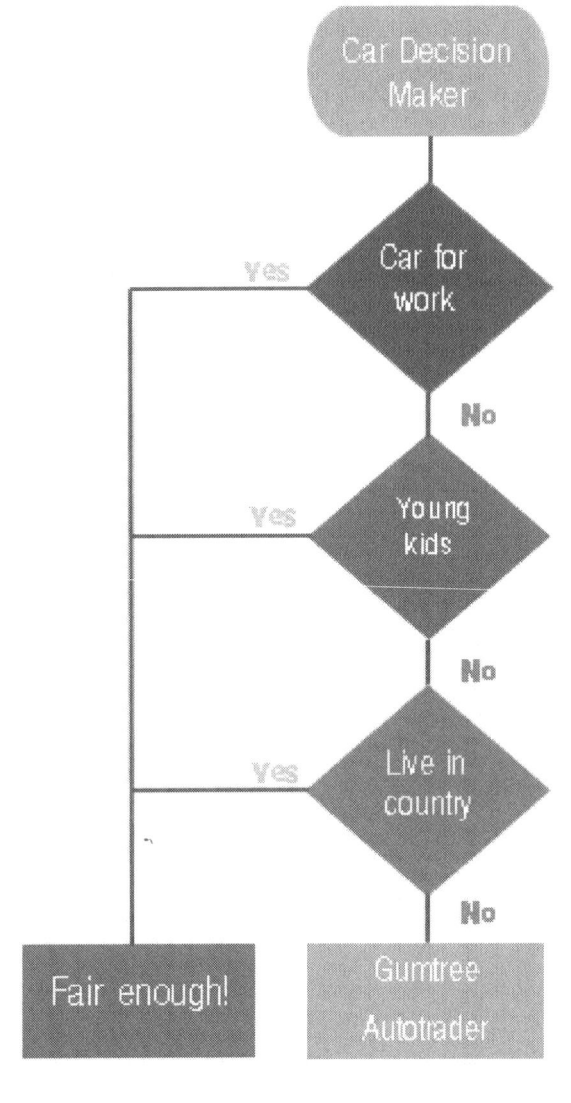

The diagram is my 'should you sell your car' decision tree. A work colleague recently bought a car. They have one 2-year-old child. They bought an estate car. Why?

"We have a growing family and we'll need it in the future". IF your family grows, trade in the cheaper supermini that you should've bought and THEN buy a bigger car if necessary. It's a bit like how parents buy expensive shoes 1 size up because they can't buy shoes at that cost too often. A few months down the line, however, the shoes become tatty and it's time for a new pair. I say buy a cheaper pair of right-fitting shoes! Yes I am opinionated, but there are a number of things that people spend their cash on that I think would be better applied to the mortgage.

I want to take you on a tour of my finances. Perhaps it's also a tour of my mindset. At the very root it's a mindset that thinks value and necessity: is buying this item worth the extra days I have to work to pay off my mortgage? First stop on the tour: eating out.

My wife is a coffee drinker but she very rarely buys coffee outside. How much is coffee these days - about £2? Let's say I have a takeaway coffee most days of the year - say 50 weeks. A daily coffee would amount to over £500 a year. Same with eating out in general. Daily lunch would be around £5 or more, right? You know what I'm going to say: that's over £1,250 a year. For me a daily take out coffee is not a necessity but I'm sure there are people out there who would swear it is. I think there are homemade or work-made alternatives. I'm not going to spend my time debating it with you! At the end of the day it's a choice. Maybe what I'm trying to show you in this section is that there are people like me who don't have vast incomes and choose the low path: they get their deposit, can pay off their mortgage quickly and have security. The others, I suppose, will take the high-living path and complain they can't get a deposit together or can't afford to make overpayments. Yes even take out coffee and lunches are high living in my world. There was a spot yesterday on Radio 4's You and Yours about 50 year olds who don't have a property and feel insecure and fearful about the future...

We rarely eat out - perhaps once a month - and if we do we eat fast casual and try to do it with vouchers. By fast casual I mean the chains like Pizza Express, Nandos and, new in Walthamstow, Grillstock. Pizza Express is well known for its vouchers and special offers. If vouchers are not available we choose carefully. As an example at Nandos as a family we get the Full Platter which comes with sides and 2 drinks (which we share) for £19.95. We never buy deserts at a restaurant: 1 small desert at £4 can't be justified in my opinion. We go to a nearby supermarket and buy cones for £1 or so. Another alternative is Pizza Hut delivery with a 50% discount voucher, which comes through our door fairly regularly - no need to spend more than £20. Even cheaper still, get something really special from the supermarket - it's still a sure saving on eating out. Wow that's a lot of detail! Why? Because throughout this section I'm showing you a mindset; what it takes to find that extra to put aside for the deposit or overpayments.

When we're on a day out with the kids and we didn't prepare food at home to bring along, we pop into the supermarket and buy a pack of ham or cheese slices for £1 or so, a stick of our favourite fresh bread and voila: cheese sandwiches! We brought our kids up on tap water and so we don't spend money on fizzy drinks. We might buy a large £1 pack of crisps to share or otherwise juicy bright clementines to supplement. So that costs us maybe £5 for a family lunch. Compare that to lunch at Pret A Manger or a restaurant.

I love cinema, but for me it doesn't represent good value family time. If we do go, obviously we avoid the overpriced food and buy popcorn and snacks from the local supermarket. For me the cinema is a lazy option – there are so many ways to have fun as a family for little or no money. On Sundays we do 'family time', which is time set aside for fun and games. We've done party games, board games and water pistol fights. I bought a relatively cheap projector as a birthday present to myself and we buy films cheaply from CEX or hire them from Google Play. The kids really look forward to movie time with popcorn and my rock cakes!

As a couple when we go out on a date night we either eat fast casual or at a take out that we've never tried, such as Square Pie or Tossed. As for fine dining, we never do it. On evenings like that for us the meal is not the central theme. It's the walking or the talking. Oh! You can't do fast casual and you prefer high dining - have you been paying attention???

Did you notice a theme with the prices? I believe that subconsciously I have an implicit £1 rule. I'll never buy crisps, ham, popcorn, tomatoes or free range eggs that cost more than £1. If I see that £1 sign I'm in! While we're in this vicinity, let's stop off at that sprawling neighbouring city of Shopping.

The trend these days is to shop at the discounters like Lidl or Aldi. Can't argue with that. The majority of our shopping is done at Asda. I regularly pop in to Sainsburys or Tesco; occasionally I go to Morrisons. It seems pretty clear that out of these Asda has for a long time been the cheapest. Waitrose and M&S (Marks and Spensive!) was a no-no. With our goal in mind, are you sure that the quality at Asda is so awful that it's worth spending that much more?

Shopping is our biggest regular cost and shopping online is my greatest money saving tip. You can easily stick to a budget as you have a running total and you avoid random shopping. There was a great show on the BBC called 'Eat Well for Less' (at the time of writing the episodes are still available). There were some fantastic habits such as allowing the kids to dictate the shopping by allowing them to put anything they desired into the trolley; also the haphazard shop where people thought "ooh I like the look of that!" or "that's new - I'll have some of that" or "I fancy a bit of that". I particularly like the family who bought stuff that they already had loads of in the house!

The programme shows how random unplanned shopping leads to a weekly family shop of up to £200 or more. Recently Carla has started planning interesting dinners for each day of week and spends no more than around £70 on the weekly online shop. Plus top ups for milk and bread and we're spending maybe £100 per week on food. For me online shopping is a no brainer:

1. Eliminate kid pressure & general hassle
2. No supermarket crowds or queues
3. No wondering "do I already have that at home?"
4. Zero spending on petrol
5. Nothing to carry
6. No car park hassle
7. Eliminate haphazard shopping
8. Stick to a budget

If you haven't already, give it a try! Next stop on our tour is our Budget. Let's talk about my general budget. Better still, I'll show you my budget!

Item	£Amount	Debit Date
Council Tax	108.00	22nd
Investments	100.00	20th
Broadband	2.50	20th
Credit Card	578.83	30th
Life Insurance	6.00	22nd
Gas & Electricity	65.00	22nd
Water	24.50	22nd
Boiler Cover	2.18	24th
Bank Charges	0.30	4th
Instant Access ISA	50.00	22nd
Mortgage	152.89	22nd
Car Insurance	26.68	22nd
Child trust fund 1	20.00	1st
Child trust fund 2	20.00	22nd
Mobile Phones	8.50	19th
Balance Transfer Card	15.00	28th
Car Loan	142.50	1st
Kids Clubs	23.00	30th
Carla Spending	150.00	
Orall Spending	100.00	
TOTAL	1595.88	

This shows our monthly expenditure and was a useful tool in getting to our target. How does it compare with your expenses? We'll go into the individual items in a minute. I combined this with another section which shows money coming in. Its main purpose was show me on payday how much I'll have left over for overpayments. I didn't have to wait until all the bills were paid, then see what was left *and then* make the overpayment: I could immediately see on payday how much I'd have left and make the payment straight away. Remember: a delay in making overpayments means extra interest!

Its second obvious purpose is analysis and control. It allowed me to monitor expenditure and alert me to how much we were spending and where. A high credit card bill this month? I'd drill down and maybe find out that we ate out more times than we'd like and so consider reducing eating out the following month. This 'budget' was a useful tool, but possibly also my biggest failing. Budgets should really be used to control spending and set limits. Initially we didn't use it in this way. Take credit card spending for example. We'd spend on the card and then get a shock at the end of the month and try to do better the following month. What we should've been doing is create a proper budget (look for resources online) set targets for spending, use the CAP Money cash system (look it up or join a CAP course), forget credit cards and withdraw a set amount of cash for the month. You see: we didn't do everything right! This would've taken months off our mortgage.

Let's now stop off at Energyville! You might have noticed from the spreadsheet that our energy costs are quite low. Annually we spend around £650 for gas and electricity (whereas the national average is £1264). How do we do it? There are 2 obvious components. Firstly get the cheapest energy deal. It's obvious but millions don't and I'm not sure why, even though the government bends over backwards to make it as easy as possible. It takes about 10 minutes. From your bill or a phone call to your supplier you need your annual consumption in Kwh and the name of your tariff. That's it! You also need to know your postcode and how you pay for your energy, but I really, really, really do hope you know these already! You then input this info into uswitch.com or other comparison site and you can switch there. You need to check you're on the cheapest deal fairly regularly (at least every 6 months or when you get your bill) because your supplier won't tell you.

Second obvious component to low energy bills is using energy wisely. Some things we do:

- ✓ Switch off the router when not in use
- ✓ We don't have a TV
- ✓ Kids switch off lights in the room when leaving
- ✓ A digital heating thermostat set at 18-19C
- ✓ Nothing on standby
- ✓ A+ efficiency rated appliances and bulbs
- ✓ Careful kettle filling & gas usage

Many people are shocked when they find out we don't have a TV - "how can you cope without it?" Well, my kids play with each other, read, draw or write stories and I have a number of interests on the go. I like learning languages, I play saxophone, I'm doing a college course and am writing this book amongst other things. Not having a TV also means I don't have a TV licence (another saving). Don't get me wrong - we use on demand services via laptops and tablets so we're not exactly TV free (I personally think this is the future of TV and not sure why TVs still exist). But I have strong views on the media and I think its controlling and influencing forces can be harmful.

Good News

I don't have a telly, but I visited my mum yesterday and watched News at 10 on hers. Top stories – school girl murderer convicted; one of the conjoined twins die; Queen's speech marred by Damian Green affair; home repossessions on the up; Ford, Chrysler and General Motors under threat of bankruptcy; mother dies being dragged under her own car. Isn't there any good news in the world? Surely someone must have done something good yesterday: someone made money, someone contributed to society in a positive way, invented something really cool or saved someone's life.

Terrorism, murder, scandal, loss. It's no surprise that people are afraid. The news is where people get a good deal of their information from and it's no surprise that they think that our government is in a state of collapse, a terrorist or some stranger or the NHS is going to kill you and you could well lose your job and your house tomorrow.

I really believe that the looming recession would be far more shallow if the news media didn't talk it up. For them the greater the tragedy, the better. You can hear the disappointment when a tragedy (e.g. plane crash) doesn't turn out so tragic after all (no fatalities). As a consolation, however, they can still speculate on how bad it might've been ('could have led to death on an unprecedented scale'). Scum. If you turn off the TV, shut the newspaper and actually look around you, the reality is that life is mostly quite uneventful.

Yesterday I left my mortgaged house for my job, didn't get killed or stabbed and didn't get blown up. The trains ran fine. During the day I didn't see any obvious signs of the government fiddling my balls and I worked, got paid and went back to my mortgaged house (curiously, it hadn't been repossessed), where I didn't murder my family. In fact, they weren't dead – my wife was doing some work and my kids were asleep.

Orall Cornelius 2008

Let's take a holiday! We'll take a short break from the commute around my finances and look at vacations. Holidays are expensive but necessary. If you have to go abroad book early and pick your time. I find the discussion about school holiday prices and permission to take kids out of school annoying. If you don't plan, don't know price patterns, are ignorant of web resources and do things last minute you will get stung. It is possible to holiday cheaply. For example, I've found Skyscanner very useful for flights and Tripadvisor good for finding quality low cost places to stay.

But ask yourself: do you really need to go abroad? We learned a good lesson from our most expensive holiday to do date: California. Ahhh California - my favourite place in the world! We went to LA, Yosemite National Park (the heart of my very favourite place in the world), San Francisco and down the coast to Monterey and Malibu. Heaven! All in all we spent perhaps £5000 on that holiday (what an overpayment that would've been)! Not a cheap holiday. But guess where our kids were happiest - was it the pricey Disneyland Hollywood or Universal

Studios? No: playing in the sand on Santa Barbara beach! If you think about it, it could've been sand anywhere: Southend or Cornwall. Point is, kids don't need you to spend loads of money on a holiday to be happy. Just a thought.

Staying with that theme, are you sure you need to go abroad? Some of our best holidays have been 'staycations': holidays in England. I'm not sure I agree with people who say they can be just as expensive as going abroad. Last year we booked a very nice Premier Inn in Nottingham (the year before that Bournemouth and before that Norfolk) at around £65 a night and had a great time. Have you experienced the cultures and sights in all parts of our great isles: Scotland, Ireland, Wales? I haven't been to Liverpool or Newcastle and we have never been camping as a family. These are next on my list.

Right, back on the bus! Let's look at general purchases such as household appliances, technology, clothes and cars. How did we choose our car? We chose it in the same way we choose everything: find the car or product with the highest rating from the most number of people at the lowest price. I'm no respecter of brand. If 400 people give a cheap no-name product 4.5 stars I'll choose it over a higher priced brand name with 3 stars any day. That goes

(386) | QUICK VIEW

Steamworks Signature Steam Iron.

£10.99

ADD TO TROLLEY

for cars, hotels, laptops or anything. Sites like Trip Advisor, Amazon and Argos make finding cheap quality items simple. Our latest car is not a flashy marque like VW, Audi or BMW. It's a relatively cheap supermini but is What Car, Car Buyer and BBC Top Gear car of the year. Easy!

We've arrived at one of my favourite towns: Phone Valley. At the time of writing the popular iPhone 6 can cost over £600. Alternatively you can get it on contract for £50-£60 per month. If you choose your phone according to my review & price rule above, you will be buying a Motorola Moto G or Moto E for £150 or £110 respectively. You'll be getting it on SIM only on a short contract so you can switch to a better deal as you wish. You might have noticed looking at the spreadsheet above that I spend £8.50 on Talk Talk mobile SIM only for both my and my wife's phones. For one phone that's £60 vs the iPhone's £600 a year.

While we're at the shopping mall let's talk clothes. Again, brand doesn't get my respect. For sportswear it has to be Sports Direct. For clothing Primark, otherwise New Look or H&M for a good balance between quality and price. I notice that there are some really good value online retailers sprouting up all over the place, especially for womenswear. Just like iPhones or fine dining, if you're serious about getting your deposit or making overpayments it's difficult to justify going much off this path.

One piece of wisdom I picked up along the road on my journey, underlying my mentality, is that consuming doesn't bring lasting happiness. You may say that you know that already, but do your shopping habits reflect that? Shininess is only temporary!

New Trainers

Have you experienced the 'new trainers' effect? Yeah, you know – when you buy that new pair of trainers, all gleaming and bright: there's no way you're gonna mess them up. Mind out mate, don't step on my trainers! Gotta avoid that puddle. And it's not only trainers; it applies to anything new: cars, phone, furniture. Absolutely no food in the car!

Then gradually, after a surprisingly short period of time wearing your trainers, you somehow don't give a crap about them! Eventually you're wearing some scruffy, dirty, smelly pair of trainers – until, of course, you get some new ones...

Orall Cornelius 2002

Think about that the next time you're feeling low and go on a spree, or before you buy that iPhone6 or Audi car.

The town of Debtville I don't visit too much. I have some debt, but here the theme is 0%. So I have a credit card debt that's on a 15 month 0% APR balance transfer deal. Our car is financed with a large deposit and 3-year 0% APR finance. I had a 0% overdraft facility of £500, which I put toward the mortgage. I have one 'buy now pay later' store card and one credit card which I clear in full on the due date, so no interest is charged. Regarding debt, I believe the wisdom is to prioritise and pay off any loans in order of highest interest rate descending – again, seek guidance from CAP or Citizens Advice. In summary, high interest loans? Avoid. Let's take an exit.

You'll notice I have an entry for ISA savings in the budget sheet. I realised that I was so fixed on overpayments that I didn't put much money aside. Fact was I still had a mortgage and so what would happen if I lost my job? Carla had an income so it wouldn't be the end of the world. I decided anyway to put £100 each month into savings. You would need to adjust that depending on risk. If Carla didn't have an income I might have put more in.

That reminds me about something I forgot to discuss: dead money. In a way I put as little into savings as I felt comfortable with. Why? Because as far as I was concerned the savings were dead money. So was money hanging about in the current account or in my pocket. For me it had to be doing something. It had to be in the mortgage or in savings: nothing else. If I got birthday money or income from eBay (we did quite a bit of eBay decluttering) it would go straight into the mortgage, no matter how small. Having both a bank account and mortgage with HSBC was convenient as I could easily view the current account and mortgage account and instantly make transfers between the two. By the way, I'm certainly not advocating you getting a mortgage from your bank! You need to search the whole market for the best deal. This was just a sort of convenient coincidence. Because of my attitude to dead money I would use savings to pay for holidays and other large expenses. If I felt savings were too large in relation to the risk in my circumstances I would move them to the mortgage.

Staying in the vicinity of savings, where should you put your money? My answer was a split between an instant access cash ISA paying the highest monthly interest I could get and a simple stock market tracker fund. If you invest in latter after a major shock (as in 2001 bottoming out in 2003

FTSE 100 Chart

Source: Google Finance

or 2008 bottoming out in 2009) this, for me, is the only sure way to make money in stocks and shares. Regular monthly saving via direct debit takes away issues relating to timing. The key risk is how long it takes the market to recover – coincidentally about 4 years from the bottom in both cases I mentioned - but there's no certainty in that. I didn't invest in any fancy investments, just a low cost UK index tracker, because other investments didn't offer value for money.

Playing Footsie

I have given my money to a selection of fund managers in the hope that they will somehow make it grow. They choose the specific shares in which to invest my money, for which I pay them an annual fee. Now, there is another way of investing. You can invest in an index tracker fund, where your cash buys a representative basket of shares from the FTSE100, FTSE250 or FT All Share indexes. There is no 'active fund manager' as such, and so consequently there's a much lower annual fee.

Very often I receive news that my actively managed shares (managed by a fund manager, who takes a higher fee remember) has under-performed the computer controlled index fund where there is no fund manager (and has a lower fee). This begs a simple question: what the hell are we paying the fund manager for? We pay them to fly business class, have lunch at the best restaurants with various CEOs, go to centre court at Wimbledon in a corporate hospitality box to drink champagne and then under-perform, that's what.

I propose a solution. Where the active fund manager under-performs the computer controlled benchmark index fund, the active fund manager takes no fee. Where they beat the index they get their fee. Fair and simple.

Orall Cornelius 2008

When I saw that the market had reached what I thought was a peak - i.e. the highest it's been in its recent history

- I cash in and transfer to the mortgage, the benefit being that the investment was acting as security savings when I had them and when I cash in I've made a little money from the market.

That's it for this part of the journey, the final stop. This was my mentality. If you want to go further in terms of saving money you can't go wrong with moneysavingexpert.com. I checked this whenever I had to get car insurance, was going on holiday, switching energy and so on and so on. This was my lifestyle when I had a mortgage. I'm not saying you have to live like this but I wanted to show you that there's an alternative lifestyle to the one where people think they are entitled to a high spending lifestyle and think what they are doing is normal. You are entitled to that but you won't get a deposit for your house or you won't make overpayments. This applies particularly to the "poor young people who can't get on the housing ladder". It seems to me that they expect to get on the ladder without sacrifice or discipline; that getting on the ladder should be on a plate. It makes me cross that people, especially the young, think they should be able to eat out, holiday, not give a second thought to spending AND expect to be helped by government or whoever to buy a home. Who said it should be easy? It's a mindset and if you want that property you need to realise it's a different lifestyle, until you get to my position. Let's get real. When you're mortgage free you can buy your take out coffee and your cake and eat it.

chapter seven

LIVING THE DREAM?

Nobody trips over mountains. It is the small pebble that causes you to stumble. Pass all the pebbles in your path and you will find you have crossed the mountain.

Tamil Proverb

In the last section I showed you some of the choices we made to get to our target. I can see perfectly the conflict in your mind: that's not my lifestyle; I can't see myself living like that. I suppose in the end it's a balance and there are extremes. I know a dad, David, at the school and he couldn't believe that we didn't have a TV and some of the other things that he treats his lads to. Playstations, Xbox and Sky TV packages. He lives a pretty carefree lifestyle, which in a way I admire. However, it costs. In nearly the same sentence he complained that he's fed up with working so hard and is finding it difficult to see how he can cope with another 24 years in the job - the time it will take him to finish his mortgage. Trapped. Then there's the other extreme: watching every penny, never eating out, never going on holiday, low price clothes and smartprice food. Trapped.

That will get you to the target really soon - if you don't get divorced before that! Yes there have been times when I've been really extreme in my money saving. Weighing the pasta servings precisely, hawkeye on the heating, comments on every purchase my wife made and lock down when the credit card bill was unexpectedly high. Looking back, I really put our marriage to the test!

There are 2 key lessons from this. First is to have buy-in from your partner. You need to be on the same page. Sell the sizzle, show the vision and make tangible the freedom and security that will come when you've met the target. A bar or line chart on the wall showing mortgage progress (and perhaps also savings and debt) is another good idea. Secondly, lighten up! If it's been a while, you can go on that holiday. If your partner has been buying-in to the plan then they deserve those shoes - they're contributing to the target too! Maybe you can celebrate or take the gas off a little when you reach a significant milestone. It's about balance.

Maybe you yourself have difficulty buying in to the mentality and lifestyle. A sociology lesson at school taught me something that stuck with me. It was related to deferred gratification. Delayed or deferred gratification is associated with resisting a smaller but more immediate reward in order to receive a larger or more enduring reward later. My sociology textbook said that there were

social class differences in that the working
delay gratification and this accounted
outcomes. I was a member of the worki
book was talking about me! I was determined
be different. If I put off the flash car and other
unnecessary spending I could have something more valuable in the longer term. Freedom!

One other reflection. There were times when I felt I wasn't living the dream. Each month I would get a feeling of joy and hope seeing the outstanding amount and monthly interest diminish. I've broken the 200k barrier, then 150k, now 100k. I found, however, that I was living for this monthly high, this fix. I didn't have much joy in anything else and maybe this focus contributed to that. Doing just enough in my work, the job became more and more a struggle and a means to an end. I was jabbing the punch bag, rather than punching through. How to combat that? Susan Jeffers, author of 'Feel the Fear and Do It Anyway', would say work your job and live the various components of your life as if your contribution matters.

chapter eight

WHAT NEXT?

"They say a person needs just three things to be truly happy in this life: someone to love, something to do, and something to look forward to"

Elvis Presley

For seven years I was focused on that monthly high. I had always dreamed of reaching the sub-10k target and now I was there. This was so much a part of my life: my life's goal. Then about a year out from target I started to wonder what I would do with my life when the target was achieved. I'd heard people talk about 'fear of success' and thought it was a ridiculous notion. But here I was experiencing it: what do I do with my life now? Should I quit my job and immerse myself in one of my many pie in the sky pipe dream projects, buy another house or move house? This took me by surprise because I always imagined that I had it planned out. Combine this with approaching middle age and uncertainty around my spiritual beliefs, it made for some major turmoil!

I'm still in the middle of that turmoil but I think I'm getting closer to working it out. Self-knowledge is the key. The most helpful question for me has been, "what are your super-strengths: what do you do better than anyone else or what do you find easier to do than anyone else?" For me the answer was writing. Tutors, work colleagues and others have always complimented me on my writing. I could combine this with my other passions, which include personal finance and using money wisely. What's your passion? I saw a useful video on YouTube that said to try lots of different things and find out what you're passionate about. So be a 'Yes' person: whenever someone asks you to do something or an interesting opportunity presents itself (especially one that's out of your comfort zone) say "Yes" and give it a go!

A personality questionnaire confirmed what I suspected: I'm an innovator and entrepreneur. I love having an idea – they're usually off the wall – and carrying it through (I'm sure I mentioned the Gentleman's Friend earlier, didn't I)? The mortgage is paid, Carla has an income well sufficient to cover expenses and even put some money aside, therefore I don't need to work. I always imagined that I would continue working and saving cash to increase the freedom, but continuing for the same company doing the same thing doesn't appeal. So I quit my job to innovate.

The decision to quit after 11 years was agonising, but 2 principles pushed me across the line. There's a military maxim that states, "the boldest moves are the safest". I try to live my life according to this.

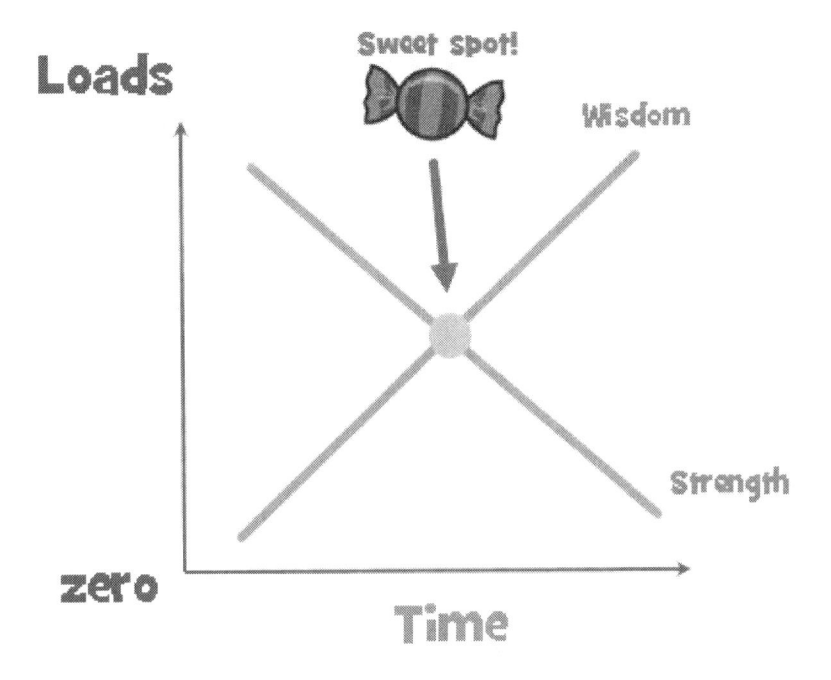

I am conscious of the passing of time and I feel I'm at that sweet spot on the continuum between naivety on the one hand and wisdom on the other, intersecting with physical health on one side and frailty on the other. Secondly, we should see the universe not as fearful place but trust that it will always deliver good, so says Susan Jeffers. According to her theory the choice we make in the end is not life critical and can always be corrected.

So that's it. The end of the ride. Hope you found it helpful and I wish you all the best on your journey to freedom!

REFERENCES

Bank of England
http://www.bankofengland.co.uk

Christians Against Poverty (CAP)
https://capuk.org

Citizens Advice Bureau
https://www.citizensadvice.org.uk

Feel the Fear & Do It Anyway
Susan Jeffers: ISBN-13:978-0091907075

Google Finance
https://www.google.co.uk/finance

Money Saving Expert
http://www.moneysavingexpert.com

uSwitch
http://www.uswitch.com

By the way, our house is now valued at around £450,000 so maybe it wasn't such a bad purchase after all…

Printed in Poland
by Amazon Fulfillment
Poland Sp. z o.o., Wrocław